D1486352

POEMS ABOUT THE WEATHER

WHO HAS SEEN THE WIND?

CHOSEN BY WENDY COOLING

Illustrated by Rowan Barnes-Murphy

W

FRANKLIN WATTS
NEW YORK•LONDON•SYDNEY

First published in 2000 by Franklin Watts
96, Leonard Street, London EC2A 4XD

Franklin Watts Australia
14 Mars Road, Lane Cove, NSW 2066

© in this anthology Wendy Cooling 2000
Illustrations © Rowan Barnes-Murphy 2000

Editor: Sarah Snashall
Designer: Louise Thomas
Art director/cover design: Jonathan Hair
Border artwork: Diana Mayo

A CIP catalogue record for this book
is available from the British Library.

ISBN 0 7496 3481 2

Dewey classification 821.008

Printed in Hong Kong/China

Acknowledgments

The editor and publishers gratefully acknowledge
permission to reproduce the following copyright material.

Weathers, by Michael Harrison. From *Junk Mail*, by
Michael Harrison, Oxford University Press. *Sunflakes*, by
Frank Asch. © 1979 Frank Asch. By permission of
Greenwillow Books, a division of William Morrow and
Co. Inc. *Happy Haiku*, by James Kirkup. Reprinted by
permission of the author. *The Wind*, by James Reeves. ©
James Reeves, from *Complete Poems for Children*
(Heinemann) by James Reeves. Reprinted by permission of
the James Reeves Estate. *Maggie and Milly and Molly and
May*, by E. E. Cummings. Reprinted from *Complete
Poems 1904-1962*, by E. E. Cummings, edited by George
J. Firmage, by permission of W. W. Norton and Company.
© 1991 by the Trustees for the E. E. Cummings Trust and
George James Firmage. *Haiku*, by Wendy Cope. Reprinted
by permission of the author. *The Sun*, by Grace Nichols.
From *Come Into My Tropical Garden* (A. & C. Black
1988). Reproduced by permission of Curtis Brown Ltd,
London, on behalf of Grace Nichols. © Grace Nichols
1988. *Spring Sunshine*, by Tony Mitton. David Higham
Associates Limited for by Tony Mitton. © Tony Mitton
1994. *There's a Murmur*, by Tony Bradman. Reproduced
by permission of The Agency (London) Ltd. © Tony
Bradman 1989. First published by Puffin Books in *All
Together Now!* All rights reserved and enquiries to The
Agency (London) Ltd, 24 Pottery Lane, London W11 4LZ
fax: 020 7727 9037. *Fog*, by Carl Sandburg. From
Chicago Poems, by Carl Sandburg. © 1916 by Holt,
Rinehart and Winston and renewed 1944 by Carl
Sandburg. Reprinted by permission of Harcourt, Inc.
Death of a Snowman, by Vernon Scannell. Reprinted by
permission of the author. *Storm*, by Roger McGough.
From *After the Merrymaking*, Cape. Reprinted by
permission of The Peters Fraser and Dunlop Group on
behalf of Roger McGough. *Hurricane*, by James Berry.
Reprinted by permission of The Peters Fraser and Dunlop
Group on behalf of James Berry. *Sea Timeless Song*, by
Grace Nichols. From *The Fat Black Woman's Poems*
(Virago Press, 1984). Reproduced by permission of Curtis
Brown Ltd, London, on behalf of Grace Nichols. © Grace
Nichols 1984. *Early in the Morning*, by Charles Causley.
From *Early in the Morning*, published by Macmillan.
Reprinted by permission of David Higham Associates. *A
Hot Day*, by A. S. J. Tessimond. Reprinted by permission
of Sadie Williams.

Every effort has been made to trace copyright, but if any
omissions have been made please let us know in order that
we may put it right in the next edition.

CONTENTS

WHAT'S THE WEATHER ON ABOUT?

What's the weather on about?
Why is the rain so down on us?
Why does the sun glare at us so?

Why does the hail dance so prettily?
Why is the snow such an overall?
Why is the wind such a tearaway?

Why is the mud so fond of our feet?
Why is the ice so keen to upset us?
Who does the weather think it is?

by Gavin Ewart

WHETHER

Whether the weather be fine
Or whether the weather be not
Whether the weather be cold
Or whether the weather be hot –
We'll weather the weather
Whatever the weather
Whether we like it or not!

Anon

WEATHERS

Weathers are moody:
Hyperactive Wind
is never still;
Wet Fog
just hangs around;
Ebullient Hail
bounces back.

Rain doesn't muck about:
he's down to earth.

by Michael Harrison

SUNFLAKES

If sunlight fell like snowflakes,
gleaming yellow and so bright,
we could build a sunman,
we could have a sunball fight,
we could watch the sunflakes
drifting in the sky.
We could go sleighing
in the middle of July
through sundrifts and sunbanks,
we could ride a sunmobile,
and we could touch sunflakes –
I wonder how they'd feel.

by Frank Asch

HAPPY HAIKU

Swimming in the rain
in summer pools – trudging through
deep snows at Christmas.

Holding fresh-baked bread
in my cold hands, then taking
the first bite – with jam.

The rainy playground –
riding my bicycle with
an umbrella up.

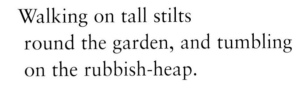

Walking on tall stilts
round the garden, and tumbling
on the rubbish-heap.

Playing in the band,
blowing my trumpet, trying
to drown the bass drum.

Knitting a muffler –
blue, purple, green, orange stripes –
knitting a muffler.

Practising kung-fu,
leap like a tiger, sideways,
kicking a long leg.

Reading by the fire,
turning the pages quickly
to the very end.

by James Kirkup

CLOTHES ON THE WASHING LINE

On windy days
Mum puts the washing on the line;
I think it's fun to watch
as she hangs Dad's shirts
upside down
and they wave their arms about
in a crazy sort of protest.
Mum's dresses always look
as though they're dancing,
but when I see my clothes
hanging on the line:
my favourite jeans
with patches on the knees,
my Liverpool football jersey
with a number seven on the back,
and a pair of grey football socks
that are supposed to be white,
it's like seeing bits of me
hanging there on the washing line.
I'm not really sure I like seeing
my clothes flapping in the wind,
I can't help feeling that I'm not altogether myself
and that I'm watching parts of me
waving me to join them.

by Frank Flynn

HAIKU

Wind lifts suddenly –
Balloon lurches from small hand,
Clutching nothing now.

by Neil Ferguson

9

WHO HAS SEEN THE WIND?

Who has seen the wind?
    Neither I nor you:
But when the leaves hang trembling
    The wind is passing thro'.

Who has seen the wind?
    Neither you nor I:
But when the trees bow down their heads
    The wind is passing by.

by Christina Rossetti

THE WIND

I can get through a doorway without any key,
And strip the leaves from the great oak tree.

I can drive storm-clouds and shake tall towers,
Or steal through a garden and not wake the flowers.

Seas I can move and ships I can sink;
I can carry a house-top or the scent of a pink.

When I am angry I can rave and riot;
And when I am spent, I lie quiet as quiet.

by James Reeves

11

MAGGIE AND MILLY AND MOLLY AND MAY

maggie and milly and molly and may
went down to the beach(to play one day)

and maggie discovered a shell that sang
so sweetly she couldn't remember her troubles,and

milly befriended a stranded star
whose rays five languid fingers were;

and molly was chased by a horrible thing
which raced sideways while blowing bubbles:and

may came home with a smooth round stone
as small as a world and as large as alone.

For whatever we lose(like a you or a me)
it's always ourselves we find in the sea.

by E. E. Cummings

HAIKU

Shimmering heat waves,
A hot pebble in the hand,
Light-dance on the sea.

by Wendy Cope

THE SUN

The sun is a glowing spider
that crawls out
from under the earth
to make her way across the sky
warming and weaving
with her bright old fingers
of light.

by Grace Nichols

APRIL RAIN SONG

Let the rain kiss you.
Let the rain beat upon your head with silver liquid drops.
Let the rain sing you a lullaby.

The rain makes still pools on the sidewalk.
The rain makes running pools in the gutter.
The rain plays a little sleep-song on our roof at night –

And I love the rain.

by Langston Hughes

SPRING SUNSHINE

Drenching the pavement,
warming the wall,
bathing the cat
in a slumbering sprawl.

Shining the shell
on a beetle's back.
Feeding the weed
that springs from a crack.

Waking the buds
that break from the tree.
Shaking out gold,
and all for free.

by Tony Mitton

EARLY SUMMER

A stone bridge, a thatched cottage,
    a crooked ford;
Swiftly, swiftly the water flows
    between its two banks.
A bright sun, a warm breeze,
    the breath of the wheatfields;
This green shade and peaceful turf
    are better than the time of flowers.

by Wang An-Shih

16

RAIN IN SUMMER

How beautiful is the rain!
After the dust and heat,
In the broad and fiery street,
In the narrow lane,
How beautiful is the rain!
How it clatters along the roofs,
Like the tramp of hoofs!

How it gushes and struggles out
From the throat of the
         overflowing spout!
Across the window pane
It pours and pours;
And swift and wide,
With a muddy tide,
Like a river down the
         gutter roars
The rain, the welcome rain!

by Henry Wadsworth Longfellow

There's a Murmur

There's a murmur
In the garden
It's the sound
Of several bees
Humming there
And buzzing
Around our apple tree

There's a murmur
In the garden
It's the sound
Of granny's snores
She's lying
In a deckchair
(And she's showing
Us her drawers)

There's a murmur
In the garden
It's the bees
They're getting close
Getting near
Her mouth now...
One's landed
On her nose

There's a silence
In the garden
We're all waiting
Holding breath...
Will the bee
Sting granny?
We're all scared
To death...

There's a murmur
In the garden
It's the sound
Of one small bee
Leaving granny's
Snoring face
Settling on
Her knee

by Tony Bradman

SUMMER DAYS

Sun's hot
Feet are blazing,
Shoes are sticking
Feel like lazing.

Faces sweating
Hot all round
Cool drinks
There I found.

In the garden
People sitting
Kids running
Grans knitting.

Summer days
Are really nice
Hot days –
Bring some ice.

by Bital Patel (aged 13)

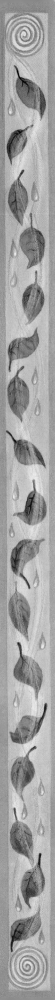

THE SUN AND FOG CONTESTED

The Sun and Fog contested
The Government of Day –
The Sun took down his yellow whip
And drove the Fog away.

by Emily Dickinson

20

FOG

The fog comes
on little cat feet.

It sits looking
over harbour and city
on silent haunches
and then moves on.

by Carl Sandburg

FOG IN NOVEMBER

Fog in November, trees have no heads,
Streams only sound, walls suddenly stop
Half-way up hills, the ghost of a man spreads
Dung on dead fields for next year's crop.
I cannot see my hand before my face,
My body does not seem to be my own,
The world becomes a far-off, foreign place,
People are strangers, houses silent, unknown.

by Leonard Clark

WINTER WALK

go.
to
like
would
we
where
show
snow
the
in
Footsteps

By Patricia Leighton

SNOWCAT

The snow is a cat,
padding softly, quietly, on all fours.
It falls with no sound,
it gives no warning of its coming,
but pounces when you least expect it.
Then,
when it has come,
it lies and suns itself,
and disappears on its rounds.

Then back at your door,
a stray cat,
an unwanted cat,
swirling around,
spitting and scratching.
Angry,
but lonely.

by Clare Fielden (aged 10)

CYNTHIA IN THE SNOW

It sushes.
It hushes
The loudness in the road.
It flitters-twitters,
And laughs away from me.
It laughs a lovely whiteness,
And whitely whirs away,
To be
Some otherwhere,
Still white as milk or shirts.
So beautiful it hurts.

by Gwendolyn Brooks

DEATH OF A SNOWMAN

I was awake all night,
Big as a polar bear,
Strong and firm and white.
The tall black hat I wear
Was draped with ermine fur.
I felt so fit and well
Till the world began to stir
And the morning sun swell.
I was tired, began to yawn;
At noon in the humming sun
I caught a severe warm;
My nose began to run.
My hat grew black and fell,
Was followed by my grey head.
There was no funeral bell,
But by tea-time I was dead.

by Vernon Scannell

STORM

They're at it again
the wind and the rain
It all started
when the wind
took the window
by the collar
and shook it
with all its might
Then the rain
butted in
What a din
they'll be at it all night
Serves them right
if they go home in the morning
and the sky won't let them in

by Roger McGough

HOW TO BEHAVE IN A THUNDERSTORM

Beware of an oak
It draws the stroke;
Avoid the ash,
It courts the flash;
Creep under the thorn,
It will keep you from harm.

Traditional

THE STORM

See lightning is flashing,
The forest is crashing,
The rain will come dashing,
   A flood will be rising anon;

The heavens are scowling,
The thunder is growling,
The loud winds are howling,
   The storm has come suddenly on!

But now the sky clears,
The bright sun appear,
Now nobody fears,
   But soon every cloud will be gone.

by Sara Coleridge

THUNDER

I hear
the drummers
strike
the sky.

by Glenys Van Every

27

HURRICANE

Under low black clouds
the wind was all
speedy feet, all horns and breath,
all bangs, howls, rattles,
in every hen house,
church hall and school.

Roaring, screaming, returning,
it made forced entry, shoved walls,
made rifts, brought roofs down,
hitting rooms to sticks apart.

It wrung soft banana trees,
broke tough trunks of palms.
It pounded vines of yams,
left fields battered up.

Invisible with such ecstasy
with no intervention of sun or man –
everywhere kept changing branches.

Zinc sheets are kites.
Leaves are panic swarms.
Fowls are fixed with feathers turned.
Goats, dogs, pigs,
all are people together.

Then growling it slunk away
from muddy, mossy trail and boats
in hedges and cows, ratbats, trees,
fish, all dead in the road.

by James Berry

SEA TIMELESS SONG

Hurricane come
and hurricane go
but sea ... sea timeless
    sea timeless
    sea timeless
    sea timeless
    sea timeless.

Hibiscus bloom
then dry-wither so
but sea ... sea timeless
    sea timeless
    sea timeless
    sea timeless
    sea timeless.

Tourist come
and tourist go
but sea ... sea timeless
    sea timeless
    sea timeless
    sea timeless
    sea timeless.

by Grace Nichols

Early in the Morning

Early in the morning
The water hits the rocks,
The birds are making noises
Like old alarum clocks,
The soldier on the skyline
Fires a golden gun
And over the back of the chimney-stack
Explodes the silent sun.

by Charles Causley

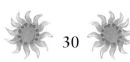

A HOT DAY

Cottonwool clouds loiter.
A lawnmower, very far,
Birrs. Then a bee comes
To a crimson rose and softly,
Deftly and fatly crams
A velvet body in.

A tree, June-lazy, makes
A tent of dim green light.
Sunlight weaves in the leaves,
Honey-light laced with leaf-light,
Green interleaved with gold.
Sunlight gathers its rays
In sheaves, which the wind unweaves
And then reweaves – the wind
That puffs a smell of grass
Through the heat-heavy, trembling
Summer pool of air.

by A. S. J. Tessimond

INDEX OF FIRST LINES

Picture credits

Cover image and title page: *Tony Stone*
(Brad Hitz)

Inside images:
Bruce Coleman p.26 (Gunter Ziesler);
Image Bank pp. 8 (Fernando Bueno), 17
(Simon Wilkinson), 20 (Terje Rakke), 22
(Joseph Van Os);
Images Colour Library pp. 4, 5, 10, 11,
24, 27, 29;
Oxford Scientific Films p.14 (Michael
Leach)
Tony Stone p.12 (Brad Hitz).